Library STEM Reader Series [Book 2]

The Alien in my Library

Is it a living or nonliving thing?

By Terrance S. Newell

SLE School Library Editions

ISBN-13: 978-0-9966099-2-0

School Library Editions
P.O. Box 11111
Milwaukee, WI 53201
http://www.SchoolLibraryEditions.com

Welcome to our **Library STEM Reader** series! This series will help your student gain success in reading, science and information skills. This is a level 1, Library STEM Reader for reading, science and information skills. This reader was designed to support every first and second grader on their journey to reading, science and information literacy. The grade levels are only guides. Students in other grades can also progress through the levels at their own individualized pace.

Level

1

Reading Skills

Reading Skills, Grades 1-2

This is a level 1, reading skills book. It is designed for early readers who can read on their own. This book features large fonts, short sentences, easy-to-follow plots and basic vocabulary for first and second graders.

Level

1

Science Content

Science Content, Grades 1-2

This is a level 1, science reader. It is designed to introduce students to first and second grade science content. This book features life science content related to the characteristics of living and nonliving things.

Level

1

Information Skills

Information Skills, Grades 1-2

This is a level 1, information skills reader. It is designed to assist students in developing AASL (American Association of School Librarians) information skills. This book features information skills related to using keywords, searching online encyclopedias, using T-charts to organize information, drawing conclusions for problem-solving and sharing information.

Four friends are working in the library.
They are learning about living and
nonliving things.

"I love working on life science projects in the library," Kenya says. "Science is very fun," replies Chris. "Let's get started!" he adds.

An alien was also working on a project in the library. Her project was to learn more about life on planet Earth.

The alien tried to move closer to the four students. "I must move quietly," the alien whispers. Then it happened! Whoosh! Oh, no!

The alien slipped! She went up into the
air. She flipped around five times.
Whoosh! Whoosh! Whoosh! Whoosh!
Whoosh! BOOM! CRASH!

The four friends could not believe their eyes. "What is it?" Chris asks. "I do not know," replies Kenya. "Hello little purple thing," Kenya says.

"Are they talking to me?" the alien
whispers. "I think they can see me," she
adds. "Should I lie here quietly, or should I
run?"

"Run!" the alien yells. "They should not see me!" she adds. "Now, I will never complete my project!" says the Alien. "I ruined the whole thing!" she yells.

"Look out!" Kenya says. "I think the purple thing is mad!" she adds. "Let's get out of here," Chris says. "Run!" Kenya yells.

CRASH! The four friends crash into the
alien. Everyone went up into the air. They
flipped around three times. Whoosh!
Whoosh! Whoosh!

"Do not eat me," Kress says as he lies on the floor. "Do not drink me," the alien says. "We will not drink you," replies Emma.

"What are you?" the alien asks. "We are humans," replies Chris. "Humans are living things," he explains. "What are you?" Chris asks.

"My name is Dewey," the alien says. "I am from a planet called Lib," she adds. "Can you tell me if I am a living thing?" Dewey asks.

"I am not sure," Chris replies. "I have a friend that could help us answer that question," Emma says. "Let's find Brie Newell!" she yells.

"Brie, I have something very strange to tell you," Emma says. "Let me guess," replies Brie. "You met an alien named Dewy that needs help?" Brie explains.

"How did you know that?" Emma asks. "It was just a guess," Brie replies. "Please excuse me," she adds. "I need to run for my life!" Brie yells.

"Run!" "Run!" "There is an alien in the library!" "Run for your lives!" Brie yells. "Wait!" yell the group.

Dewey flew across the room to stop Brie. "I will not harm you," Dewey explains. "You are very smart, and I could really use your help!" Dewey says.

Brie touches Dewey's head, and replies, "I will help you." "Thank you!" yells Dewey. "Am I a living thing?" Dewey asks.

"The library has resources that can help us answer that question," Brie explains. "Students use resources to learn more about school subjects," she adds.

"Students also use resources to learn more about their personal interests," Brie says. "Resources can be people, places, objects, technologies or printed materials," she adds.

"To answer your question, we are going to use an online encyclopedia to find information about living and nonliving things," Brie explains.

"An online encyclopedia is a resource that provides information about one or more subjects," Brie says. "We can use the internet to access an online encyclopedia."

"Let's find the information that we need,"
Brie says. "First, we need to type one or
more keywords into the encyclopedia's
long rectangular bar called a search bar."

"Keywords are the most important words related to the information that you need," Brie says. "We have to use good keywords to find good information," she explains.

"Let's type the words living thing into
the search bar," Brie suggests. "I will read
the information about living things, but I
need someone to take notes," Brie says.

"I know a great way to take notes," Kress says. "We can use a graphical organizer called a T-chart," he explains. "T-charts help students organize information," Kress says.

Things

Living	Nonliving

"A T-chart is simply a chart that looks like the letter T," Kress explains. "We can use it to compare and contrast the information about living and nonliving things," he adds.

"Great idea," Brie says. "I found information about the characteristics of living and nonliving things," she adds. "I will read the information, and you can write it on the T-Chart," Brie explains.

Things

Living	Nonliving

✓ Need food
✓ Need water
✓ Need air
✓ They reproduce
✓ They grow and
   change

"These are the 5 characteristics of living things," Brie reads. "Living things need food. Living things need water. Living things need air. Living things reproduce. Living things grow and change."

"The online encyclopedia also has information about nonliving things," Brie says. "I will read the information, and Kress can write it on the T-chart," she adds.

Things

Living	Nonliving
✓ Need food	✗ No food
✓ Need water	✗ No water
✓ Need air	✗ No air
✓ They reproduce	✗ Don't reproduce
✓ They grow and change	✗ Don't grow and change

"These are the characteristics of nonliving things," Brie reads. "Nonliving things do not need food. They do not need water. They do not need air. They do not reproduce. They do not grow and change."

"I am so happy," Emma says. "We have
the information needed to answer Dewey's
question," she adds. "Let's see if Dewey has
the characteristics of living things," cries
Emma.

"Ok, Dewey," says Brie. "We will use the T-Chart to ask you a few questions," she explains. "Your answers will tell us if you are a living or nonliving thing," she adds.

"I will ask the first question," Kenya says. "Dewey, do you need food to survive?" she asks. "Yes," Dewey replies. "I eat food every 100 days," Dewey says.

"I will ask the second question," Emma says. "Dewey, do you need water to survive?" she asks. "Yes," Dewey replies. "I use my fingers to drink rain water," Dewey explains.

"I will ask the third question," Chris says.
"Dewey, do you need air to survive?" he
asks. "Yes," Dewey replies. "I breathe
through my toes," she adds.

"Living things make new things that are similar to themselves," Kress says. "In other words, they reproduce," he explains. "Dewey, can you reproduce?" Kress asks. "Yes," Dewey replies. "I lay eggs!"

"This is the last question," Brie says.
"Dewey, do you grow and change?" she
asks. "Yes," Dewey replies. "I will be 30
feet tall in a few years," she explains.

"Living things need food, water and air."
"They also reproduce and grow." "Dewey,
you are a living thing!" Brie yells. Dewey
was so happy that she jumped on the table
and danced.

Vocabulary Review

Hi, readers! These are words that you should remember.

- ➤ **Keywords**
  - ○ The most important words related to the information that you need. You need good keywords to find good information.
- ➤ **Life Science**
  - ○ The study of living things.
- ➤ **Living Things**
  - ○ Organisms that need food, water and air to survive. They also reproduce and grow.
- ➤ **Nonliving Things**
  - ○ Organisms that <u>do not</u> need food, water and air to survive. They <u>do not</u> reproduce and grow.
- ➤ **Online Encyclopedia**
  - ○ A resource that provides information about one or more subjects.
- ➤ **Resources**
  - ○ Students use resources to learn more about academic subjects and things of personal interest. Resources can be people, places, objects, technologies or printed materials.
- ➤ **School Library**
  - ○ A library within a school. School libraries have learning resources for students.
- ➤ **T-Chart**
  - ○ A tool used to organize information. It looks like the letter T. It can be used to compare and contrast information.

www.ingramcontent.com/pod-product-compliance
Lightning Source LLC
Chambersburg PA
CBHW060632030426
42337CB00018B/3326